First World War
and Army of Occupation
War Diary
France, Belgium and Germany

1 DIVISION
3 Infantry Brigade
Queen's (Royal West Surrey Regiment)
1st Battalion
4 August 1914 - 31 December 1914

WO95/1280/1

The Naval & Military Press Ltd
www.nmarchive.com
Published in association with The National Archives

Published by

The Naval & Military Press Ltd

Unit 10 Ridgewood Industrial Park,

Uckfield, East Sussex,

TN22 5QE England

Tel: +44 (0) 1825 749494

www.naval-military-press.com

www.nmarchive.com

This diary has been reprinted in facsimile from the original. Any imperfections are inevitably reproduced and the quality may fall short of modern type and cartographic standards.

© **Crown Copyright**
Images reproduced by permission of The National Archives, London, England, 2015.

Contents

Document type	Place/Title	Date From	Date To
Heading	1Div 3 Infantry Brig WO95 1280/1 1 Btn Royal West Surrey Reg		
Heading	1st Division 3rd Infantry Brigade 1st Battalion Royal West Surrey Regiment Aug-Dec 1914 (To 2 Div 5 Bde)		
Heading	3rd Brigade. 1st Division. 1st Battalion The Royal West Surrey Regiment August 1914		
Heading	1st Division. 3rd Inf. Bde. War Diary. (Queen's) 1st Bn. The R. West Surrey Rgt. 1914 (4 August-1 September)		
War Diary	Bordon	04/08/1914	11/08/1914
War Diary	On The Move	12/08/1914	12/08/1914
War Diary	Havre	13/08/1914	14/08/1914
War Diary	On The Move	15/08/1914	15/08/1914
War Diary	Leschelles	16/08/1914	19/08/1914
War Diary	On The Move	20/08/1914	23/08/1914
War Diary	Croix Des Rouveroy	23/08/1914	23/08/1914
War Diary	On The Move	24/08/1914	01/09/1914
Heading	3rd Brigade. 1st Division. 1st Battalion The Royal West Surrey Regiment September 1914 Attached is Summary of Situation on 14th		
Heading	1st Division 3rd Inf. Bde. War Diary (Queen's) 1st Bn. The R. West Surrey Rgt. September 1914		
War Diary	On The Move	01/09/1914	13/09/1914
War Diary	Near Paissy	14/09/1914	14/09/1914
War Diary	Paissy Ridge	15/09/1914	19/09/1914
War Diary	Vendresse	20/09/1914	23/09/1914
War Diary	Nr Vendresse	24/09/1914	27/09/1914
War Diary	Oeuilly	28/09/1914	30/09/1914
War Diary	Paissy	14/09/1914	17/09/1914
War Diary	Chemin Des Dames	17/09/1914	19/09/1914
Miscellaneous	Battle of The Aisne 14th September Report By The Queen's Regiment		
Diagram etc	Maps		
Miscellaneous	A Form. Messages And Signals.		
Heading	3rd Brigade. 1st Division.1st Battalion The Queen's Royal West Surrey Regiment October 1914		
Heading	1st Division 3rd Inf. Bde. War Diary (Queen's) 1st Bn. The R. West Surrey Rgt. October 1914		
Miscellaneous	Report on Fighting. App XV	06/11/1914	06/11/1914
War Diary	Oeuilly	30/09/1914	01/10/1914
War Diary	Verneuil	02/10/1914	14/10/1914
War Diary	Courcelles	15/10/1914	16/10/1914
War Diary	On The Move	17/10/1914	17/10/1914
War Diary	Hondeghem	18/10/1914	18/10/1914
War Diary	On The Move	19/10/1914	21/10/1914
War Diary	400 S. W of Langemarck.	22/10/1914	23/10/1914
War Diary	In Trenches	24/10/1914	24/10/1914
War Diary	Hooge	24/10/1914	28/10/1914
War Diary	In Trenches E of Gheluvelt	28/10/1914	30/10/1914
War Diary	Gheluvelt	31/10/1914	31/10/1914
Miscellaneous	O.C. Queen Appx. XIV		

Map	Appendix I		
Map	Roulers		
Miscellaneous	Roulers (with Square)		
Miscellaneous	A Form. Messages And Signals.		
Diagram etc	Sketch Map of Action on Oct 23rd 1914. Appendix II		
Miscellaneous	A Form. Messages And Signals. Appendix III		
Miscellaneous	A Form. Messages And Signals. Appendix IV		
Diagram etc	Situation of Queen's on 30th & 31st Oct 1914. Appendix V		
Miscellaneous	A Form. Messages And Signals. Appendix VIII		
Miscellaneous	A Form. Messages And Signals. Appendix VII		
Miscellaneous	A Form. Messages And Signals. Appendix IX		
Miscellaneous	A Form. Messages And Signals. Appendix X		
Miscellaneous	A Form. Messages And Signals. Appendix XI		
Miscellaneous	A Form. Messages And Signals. Appendix XII		
Miscellaneous	To O.C. Queen's Appendix XIII		
Map	Maps		
Heading	3rd Brigade. 1st Division. Battalion became Corps Troops 8th November 1st Battalion The Queen's Royal West Surrey Regiment November 1914		
Heading	1st Division 3rd Inf. Bde. War Diary (Queen's) 1st Bn. The R. West Surrey Rgt. November 1914 Battalion became Corps Troops 8/11/14		
War Diary	In Trenches E of Hooge	01/11/1914	04/11/1914
War Diary	Bellewarde Farm	04/11/1914	05/11/1914
War Diary	In Trenches S of Zille Beke	05/11/1914	08/11/1914
War Diary	Brielen	09/11/1914	21/11/1914
War Diary	Hazebrouck	22/11/1914	30/11/1914
Miscellaneous	Letter From Capt. J.D. Boyd. D.S.O.		
Heading	Corps Troops File with 3rd Brigade. 1st Division. 1st Battalion The Queen's Royal West Surrey Regiment December 1914		
Heading	1st Division 3rd Inf. Bde. Corps Troops from 8/11/14 War Diary (Queen's) 1st Bn. The R. West Surrey Rgt. December 1914		
War Diary	Hazebrouck	01/12/1914	28/12/1914
War Diary	Hinges	29/12/1914	31/12/1914

WO 95

1280/1
_____

1 Bth Royal West Survey Reg

1 AN
3 Infantry Brig

1ST DIVISION
3RD INFANTRY BRIGADE

1ST BATTALION
ROYAL WEST SURREY REGIMENT
AUG - DEC 1914

(TO 2 DIV. 5 BDE)

3rd Brigade.
1st Division.

1st BATTALION

THE ROYAL WEST SURREY REGIMENT

AUGUST 1 9 1 4

1st Division
3rd Inf.Bde.

WAR DIARY

(QUEEN'S) 1st Bn. The R.WEST SURREY RGT.

1 9 1 4

(4 August — 1 September.)

Army Form C. 2118.

WAR DIARY
or
INTELLIGENCE SUMMARY.
(Erase heading not required.)

Instructions regarding War Diaries and Intelligence Summaries are contained in F.S. Regs., Part II. and the Staff Manual respectively. Title pages will be prepared in manuscript.

Hour, Date, Place	Summary of Events and Information	Remarks and references to Appendices
	The original copy of this War Diary was lost on Oct 31st together with the greater part of the Batt⁻. This copy was rewritten from the only available record which remained on 301/10⁻ and following days, namely the present diary & one of the recovery Officers, supplemented from memory.	
1914.		
BORDON 5.30 p.m Aug 4th	Received orders to mobilize.	
9.15 p.m	Conference of all officers of the Bn. to ascertain extent of readiness. Previous to this an order had been issued for an Emergency Mobilization so that a great deal of the preparations had already been completed.	
Aug 5th	First day of Mobilization. Coffins of all Officers as above.	
9.0 p.m	450 Recruits joined from Depot at 11.30 p.m.	
Aug 6th	Second day of Mobilization. 130 Recruits joined from Depot about 4 p.m.	
Aug 7th 5.0 p.m	Third day of Mobilization. Mobilization complete and same reported to 3/5 Bde H.Q.	
Aug 8th	Reveille 4+5 a.m. Half Batt⁻ at a time proceeded to Range where the following practices were fired by every man — 100 yds (grouping) and 300 yds slow and rapid	yds

(9 29 6) W 4141—463 100,000 9/14 H W V Forms/C. 2118/10

Army Form C. 2118.

WAR DIARY
or
INTELLIGENCE SUMMARY.

(Erase heading not required.)

Instructions regarding War Diaries and Intelligence Summaries are contained in F.S. Regs., Part II. and the Staff Manual respectively. Title pages will be prepared in manuscript.

Hour, Date, Place	Summary of Events and Information	Remarks and references to Appendices
BORDON. Aug 9th	Batt" exercised under the Commanding Officer in different formations at and around OXNEY FARM.	
— Aug 10th	Musketry on Range at 500 yds and practised Fire Control, Judging Distance etc under Company arrangements. In the interval of firing During the afternoon carried out an attack on WEAVERS DOWNS under the Commanding Officer.	
— Aug 11th	Batt" parade, strong as possible at 9 a.m. and went for short route march and practised formation for the preliminary stages of an attack.	
ON THE MOVE Aug 12th	Batt" paraded and marched to BORDON STA. Right half at 9.30 a.m. left half at 10.30 a.m. and embarked on S.S. BRAEMAR CASTLE. Destination unknown. Arrival at SOUTHAMPTON at 2 p.m. The WELSH REGT. shared the transport with the Batt"	
8.15 p.m	Left wharf and proceeded out of harbour, escorted at first by a destroyer. Destination still unknown.	
HAVRE Aug 13th – 11 a.m.	Arrived at HAVRE and carried Unloading of baggage, horses etc proceeded until 5.30 p.m. Marched 6 miles to CAMP NUMERO 6. Transport was obliged to sleep by another road as the way the Batt" marched was too steep. Road by another road so the way the Batt" marched was road cut. Three cheers	
HAVRE Aug 14th – 10.0 a.m.	Batt" paraded and the KING'S Speech was read out and another was given. The Commanding Officer addressed the Batt" and spoke of the probable hardships it would have to face and the manner in which the Batt" was expected to do so. Cheerfully and without grumbling. Much difficulty experienced in filling water bottles from the water Cartons This, the first occasion in which the unit had been issued of a	

Forms/C. 2118/10

WAR DIARY or INTELLIGENCE SUMMARY.

Army Form C. 2118.

(Erase heading not required.)

Hour, Date, Place	Summary of Events and Information	Remarks and references to Appendices
ON THE MOVE Aug 15th 3 a.m.	Camp mustered over. By the use of habits it was eventually formed possible to fill the water bottles of 2 platoons war strength in about 3/4 of an hour. The Battn. marched off along the ridge overlooking HAVRE and entrained at HAVRE STA. at 5.30 a.m. Left HAVRE at 9.30 a.m., Destination unknown. Passed through RUEN at 1 p.m. — where there was a half-hour halt and tea was made. Arrived at AMIENS at 7 p.m. ARRAS 10.0 p.m. and LE NOUVION at 2.30 a.m. on Aug 16th.	
LESCHELLES Aug 16th 5.30 a.m.	Marched from LE NOUVION to LESCHELLES where the Battn. went into Billets. Bn. H.Q. in CHATEAU. Settled into Billets. Outposts put out and sentries posted on Billig. Movements in the field carried out under Company arrangements. Sections a different method of challenging in French and German.	
— Aug 17th	Movements in the field and Outposts all morning under Company arrangements.	
— Aug 18th	Paraded for a B'dy Route March through BURONFOSSE and ESQUÉHERIES	
On the move Aug 19th 9.45 a.m. Aug 20th 8.0 a.m.	Battn. marched off for LESCHELLES through BARZY to LESART where the night was spent in Billets.	
— Aug 21st 7.15 a.m.	Left LE SART and marched through BEAUREPÈRE, CARTIGNIES, and DOMPIERRE to LES BOCLEZ. Paid out under Company arrangements.	
— Aug 22nd 5 a.m.	Received orders to move and marched through ST AUBIN and along road west north to MAUBEUGE. This road almost entirely in	

Forms/C. 2118/10

WAR DIARY
or
INTELLIGENCE SUMMARY.

(Erase heading not required.)

Army Form C. 2118.

Instructions regarding War Diaries and Intelligence Summaries are contained in F.S. Regs., Part II. and the Staff Manual respectively. Title pages will be prepared in manuscript.

Hour, Date, Place	Summary of Events and Information	Remarks and references to Appendices
CROIX DES ROUVEROY Aug 23rd	rough cobble streets and very trying. Battn. headquarted at 1 p.m. Resumed march at 3.30 p.m. to DB TTIGMES and after a halt continued the march at 6.45 p.m. The Battn. crossed the Belgian frontier about 7 p.m. and reached CROIX DES ROUVEROY about 8.30 p.m. where billets were occupied. The Battn. started entrenching itself at 5 a.m. on a ridge immediately North of the village. The remainder of the 3rd D.ᵒᵉ were about 600 yds in rear of our position. At 2.30 p.m. the Turks themselves had been dug and entered and was constructed. The battle of MONS had been in progress all the afternoon, and at 6.0 p.m. the Battn. received an order to reinforce the flank. After marching about a mile the Battn. was halted and lay down in reserve awaiting orders. The battle had however died down and after two hours the Battn. returned to their original line. The enemy's searchlights were fully used on the Turkish throughout the night.	Only gunfire possible at Rouveroy this morning owing to sudden orders to move. In this proper clouds were seen about 8" - 1" of earth thrown in the trap of them.
On the move. Aug 24th	Soon after dawn the 3rd D.ᵒᵉ commenced the retirement, covered by the Battn. No great enemy shelling and whether this was ever the Turks and about 300 yds behind. By 7.45 the remainder of the 3rd D.ᵒᵉ were all clear and the Battn. began to withdraw, and 3 D.ᵒᵉ were all clear and the Battn. Only one cavalry patrol of the enemy's company at a time. Only one cavalry patrol of the enemy's approached to within 400 yds and this patrol was exterminated. The shelling however much more pronounced almost immediately after the Battn. had cleared the village. Retired through BOTTIGMIES where there was a halt of 1/2 hour. Marched	

WAR DIARY
or
INTELLIGENCE SUMMARY.
(Erase heading not required.)

Army Form C. 2118.

Hour, Date, Place	Summary of Events and Information	Remarks and references to Appendices
On the move. Aug 25. 5 a.m.	The march at 1.30 a.m. and retired to NEUF MESNIL where we went into billets. Lieut Cooper left about today owing to sprained ankle. Marched off through HAUTMONT, LIMONT, ST REMY, DOMPIERRE and MARBAIX. Halted for 1 hour here. The Regt to G.H.Q. EAST where the R.A.M.C. billetted. Thence the men't march up to date.	
6 p.m.	Brigade alarmed by some rifle fire and turned out; a Cavalry patrol was reported to be in the vicinity. Considerable confusion amongst the 73rd and a good deal of firing, after occupying a position covering the village for about 2 hours, the 73rd were withdrawn into billets again. Casualties – Nil.	
On the move. Aug 26.	Reveille at 1 a.m. 3 C.O's of the Regt's Staff. Reached Mal. S. a.m. Towards FAVRIL to rejoin the 4 B.H of Brigade. The 13th occupied a position and entrenched. Facing LANDRECIES. Received the order to retire about 2 p.m and did so in the order B, C, A, D. The Dorset group who occupied the line held by the Batt. on retirement covered the three minutes of our vacating the trenches. Reached S.W. through LA GUISE to OISY arriving there at 7 p.m. Lieutenant PAIN wounded when I.O.M. transport.	Rations were drawn in the road from lorries laying open extra near of the Town. This operation was carried out almost without check.
LA GROISE O.T.A. On the move Aug 27.	Reveille 5 a.m. Marched off at 10.45 a.m. and had the longest march hitherto through GUISE, then took things — again to reinforce one of our troops. These last entrained elsewhere successfully however on recent march through GUISE to BERNOT. Reaching the latter at various small thanks in the heavy convoy 2.7 miles with no halt of 2 an hour however	Very heavy rain in the front nearly this march.

Army Form C. 2118.

WAR DIARY
or
INTELLIGENCE SUMMARY.
(Erase heading not required.)

Instructions regarding War Diaries and Intelligence Summaries are contained in F. S. Regs., Part II. and the Staff Manual respectively. Title pages will be prepared in manuscript.

Hour, Date, Place	Summary of Events and Information	Remarks and references to Appendices
On the move Aug 28th	Reveille at 4 a.m. Coy & D Company entrenched a position immediately North of the village and faring MONTIGNY. Occupied this position until 10 p.m. The Batt'n retired at 1 p.m. and the village was heavily shelled within half an hour. Continuous retirement through BERRIEMONT and LUCY to SENERCY where we halted for 2½ hours. Resumed march at 5.30 p.m. and covered 19 more miles to BARISIS. This march was the most trying of the whole retreat. The majority of it was carried out with two Battalions and transport abreast on the road. Our Batt'n actually covered 8 miles more than the necessary owing to the miscarriage of an order from 3rd Div H.Q.	Total number of miles 32 in 16½ hours with a 2½ hours halt.
— Aug 29th	Spent the day in billets up to 5 p.m. then rejoined the 3rd Division at BERTAUCOURT where the troops were renewing in bivouac.	
— Aug 30th	Marched off at 4.30 a.m. through ST GOBAIN and SEPTVAUX to BRANCOURT and went into billets there.	
— Aug 31st	Marched off at 5.40 a.m. through ANIZY LE CHATEAU and PINON, SOISSONS and bivouacced in a field close to MISSY AUX BOIS. German Cav Div'n reported to be moving on the Western front towards PARIS.	Thick fog all today.
— Sept 1st	Marched off at 6.15 through VERTE FEUILLE. After an enemy reported to be at ATTIGNY (10 miles to N.W.) and the G.O.C. called on the 3rd A.B. for a special effort today. Halted for 1½ hour at VILLERS— COTTERETS STATION. Resumed march at 1 p.m. to the S.W. through LA FERTE MILON and reached bivouac 1 mile S.E. this place at 9 p.m.	

(8 29 6) W 4141—463 100,000 9/14 H W V Forms/C. 2118/10

3rd Brigade.
1st Division.

1st BATTALION

THE ROYAL WEST SURREY REGIMENT

SEPTEMBER 1 9 1 4

Attached is summary of situation on 14th

1st Division
3rd Inf.Bde.

WAR DIARY

(QUEEN'S) 1st Bn. The R.WEST SURREY RGT.

September

1914

WAR DIARY

Copied from last page of War
Diary for August

1st Battalion the QUEENS

SEPTEMBER

On the move

Sept. 1st   Marched off at 6.15 through VERTE FEUILLE. At 8 a.m. enemy reported to be at
ATTIGNY (10 miles to N.W.) and the G.B.C. called on the 3rd Bde. for a
special effort to day. Halted for 1½ hours at VILLERS COTTERETS STATION.
Resumed march at 1 p.m. to the S.W. through LA FERTE MILON and reached
bivouac 1 mile S. of this place at 9 p.m.

WAR DIARY
or
INTELLIGENCE SUMMARY.
(Erase heading not required.)

Army Form C. 2118.

Hour, Date, Place	Summary of Events and Information	Remarks and references to Appendices
On the move Sept 2nd	Reveille 12.15 a.m. No fires permitted so marched off without food. Through VARM FROY. Halted by the roadside from 9.0 to 11 a.m. & had breakfast. Resumed march at 11.0 a.m. through VARREDES and CRÉCY to PENCHARD. Billeted here for the night.	
Sept 3rd	Reveille 2 a.m. Marched through CRECY, GERMIGNY, CHANGIS and SAMMERON where B Coy halted for 4 hours. A Company under Captn M.G. HEATH left here to guard a bridge over the R. MARNE. B Coy continued the retirement at 3 p.m. to PERREUSE where we went into Bivouac.	
Sept 4th	Reveille 2.45 a.m. Moved out of Bivouac at 4.30 a.m. outposts were withdrawn at 7 a.m. previous to resuming the march. Through PETIT COURROIS and AULNOY to MOURDUX, men tea at 3.30 p.m. A return was rendered of all men unable to proceed on the march. Tonight and 12 men were found unfit to proceed. At 5 p.m. the 2nd Division commenced to fall back through the village. The 1st Bde resumed the march at 6.30 p.m. and acted as rear guard. Proceeded about 5 miles and bivouacked in a field.	
Sept 5th	The 1st Bde continued to cover the retirement today. Marched through MAUPERTHUIS and ORMEAUX to ROZOY. Our Bn was in rear of the Bde and all stragglers were collected and kept moving. (Lieut Reinforcement) Lieut PHILLIPS joined with 90 men.	

WAR DIARY
or
INTELLIGENCE SUMMARY.
(Erase heading not required.)

Army Form C. 2118.

Instructions regarding War Diaries and Intelligence Summaries are contained in F.S. Regs., Part II. and the Staff Manual respectively. Title pages will be prepared in manuscript.

Hour, Date, Place	Summary of Events and Information	Remarks and references to Appendices
On the move Sept 6th	Reveille 5.15 a.m. Marched off at 7 a.m. The Batt. was advanced Guard. Deployed and moved in the direction of LES HAUTES GRES Farm which latter was pierced in a state of defence. Resumed the advance and at 6 p.m. advanced to take the village of VAUDOY and did so without opposition. Went into bivouac on high ground immediately N of village.	
On the move Sept 7th	Stood to arms at 4 a.m. Took up a covering position on the ridge about 500 yds to the North and occupied this line till 12.0 (noon) in relief of the 2nd R.B. Two civilian Frenchmen found dressed here and the occupants of adjoining farms were questioned. No information elicited as to the matter was reported to the local Mayor. One of them had his hands tied. Both were shot through the head for alarm. Advanced through DAGNY, CHEVRU, to COFFRY where we bivouaced for the night.	No water obtainable.
On the move Sept 8th	Marched off at 5.30 a.m. via CHOISY, LA BOULLAIS, JOUY, CAMP MARTIN, and GD MARCHÉ. Took up a position here to cover the Guards Bde Cotoneed march through HONDEVILLIERS. Remained 2½ hrs on ridge close to FERME DE L'ILE, but arrived too far in too late to participate. Lieut F.W.H. DENTON and Lieut RAWSON joined unit 91 men (2nd Reinforcements).	

Army Form C. 2118.

WAR DIARY
or
INTELLIGENCE SUMMARY.
(Erase heading not required.)

Instructions regarding War Diaries and Intelligence Summaries are contained in F.S. Regs., Part II. and the Staff Manual respectively. Title pages will be prepared in manuscript.

Hour, Date, Place	Summary of Events and Information	Remarks and references to Appendices
On the move Sept 9th	Marched off at 5 a.m. Through BASSEVELLE and SAULCHERY. Here a crossing had to be effected over a bridge. The 3rd Day was in front and dispositions were as follows:— The GLOUCESTER Regt took up a position covering the bridge on the left. Our Batt. crossed the bridge, followed by the WELSH Regt and S.W. Border Regt, who took up a position on the Ridge to our front. The crossing was carried out without opposition. Occupied a first position at BONNEIL. Advanced at 12.0 (noon) to LES AULNOIS BONTIEMPS & remained there until 3.15 p.m. when we advanced to the main road part E. of road PARIS. (MEAUX MAP.) Spent the night at LE THIOLET.	
On the move Sept 10th	Marched off at 8.10 a.m. and went to along the Road to PARIS, then N through LUCY, TORCY, and COUR CHAMPS. Here the 2nd Div. were in front and suffered heavy casualties. The 5th Divn advanced to SOMMELANS where we remained until dusk. Marched through PRIEZ to SOMMELANS & went into billets there.	
On the move Sept 11th	The Batt. marched off at 5 a.m. Through GRISOLLES, ROCOURT and COINCY to VILLENEUVE where we bivouaced in and around small farms.	

Forms/C. 2118/10

WAR DIARY
or
INTELLIGENCE SUMMARY.
(Erase heading not required.)

Army Form C. 2118.

Instructions regarding War Diaries and Intelligence Summaries are contained in F.S. Regs., Part II. and the Staff Manual respectively. Title pages will be prepared in manuscript.

Hour, Date, Place	Summary of Events and Information	Remarks and references to Appendices
On the move Sept 12th.	Reveille 4.15 a.m. Marched through FERE, LOUPEIGNE, BRUYS, and BAZOCHES. A German Column was retreating about 1½ hours march to our front along this same road and the French Artly. was shelling the column as our horse force hove Flanks. There was some delay over the deployment of the leading Reg't. on B.5t and BATTn.B was brought up to the front & deployed on the advance continued. Reached VAUXCERE at 8 p.m. The Batt. occupied billets here for the night.	
On the move Sept 13th.	Rested in billets all morning. Marched off at 2.30 p.m. through LONGUEVAL and BOURG. Here could be seen an attempt on the part of the enemy to blow up an aqueduct bridge, a party of it having been observed. after holding the column about 500 yds n/s the River AISNE. the Bat't went into billets in N.W. of the village.	
Near PAISSY. Sept 14th.	N.B.30 a.m. Marched off at 7.10 a.m. Through MOULINS to PAISSY. The Batt. was detached from the remainder of the Bde. to act as escort to our Artillery on the right flank, and next to the French. Deployed to the N.E of PAISSY and advanced in extended lines of Platoons, B and C Companies in the firing line and A+D Companies in support. No serious opposition was encountered before arriving on the line of the CHEMIN DES DAMES road.	

WAR DIARY
or
INTELLIGENCE SUMMARY.
(Erase heading not required.)

Army Form C. 2118.

Instructions regarding War Diaries and Intelligence Summaries are contained in F.S. Regs., Part II. and the Staff Manual respectively. Title pages will be prepared in manuscript.

Hour, Date, Place	Summary of Events and Information	Remarks and references to Appendices
	The advance was continued with front of a wood (about 400–500 yards N of the road). Here our left consisting of B and C Coys encountered some opposition and came under heavy rifle and M.G. fire. A bit was unsufficient their flank whilst D Coy held the front of the wood. The Nat's machine guns were unsupported bringing up on the right flank, but finding an inadequate field of fire, Lieut. PRINGLE moved them across to the left flank to assist A, B, & C Companies. In front of the enemy was advancing arms towards the right flank where the French were, and a considerable enemy casualties were caused at a range of 1100 yards. A wide valley separated our position from the enemy's main line of trenches. D Company in the N were ½ mile well concealed for view and had few casualties. At about 3 p.m. the Commanding Officer received a route attack to be made to our right flank against the enemy's flank as they advanced on to the French. Captain HUNTER with 2 Platoons of D Company proceeded to this front, but was soon unopposed & came up with attack, the enemy being by this time in considerable numbers and the French having fallen back to the line of the CHEMIN DES DAME. On our left a most severe attack was made against A, B & C Coys. (Two officers now known of these companies and details cannot have given as to the movements on this flank.)	

WAR DIARY
or
INTELLIGENCE SUMMARY.
(Erase heading not required.)

Army Form C. 2118.

Hour, Date, Place	Summary of Events and Information	Remarks and references to Appendices
	At about 4.30 p.m. the Commanding Officer directed that a retirement should be carried out to the line of the CHEMIN DES DAMES. D Coy fell back first in well extended formation, followed by H + B Coys with C Company (weaker) up the rear. Captain LONGBOURNE commanded the latter Company and brought in several of our wounded Officers and men. The Battⁿ. lay about 50 yds in front of men Battⁿ. and under heavy shell fire from the enemy until darkness came on. The following were the casualties amongst the Officers and men:— 9th Battⁿ:— Lieut. R.L.Q. Henriques killed. Major Pelham D.S.O. 2nd Lieut. Mathew-Lannowe Captain HEATH, and M^cNAMARA Lieutenants KENNY, DENTON, PRINGLE } Wounded W. HAYES and BUSHELL 13 N.C.O's and men killed and 88 wounded 39 N.C.O's and men missing.	

Army Form C. 2118.

WAR DIARY
or
INTELLIGENCE SUMMARY.
(Erase heading not required.)

Instructions regarding War Diaries and Intelligence Summaries are contained in F.S. Regs., Part II. and the Staff Manual respectively. Title pages will be prepared in manuscript.

Hour, Date, Place	Summary of Events and Information	Remarks and references to Appendices
PAISSY RIDGE. Sept 15th Sept 16th Sept 17th Sept 18th	2 Companies entrenched all night in the line of the CHEMIN DES DAMES road and 2 Companies remained in support in hollow about 800 yds in rear. Shelled over after dawn. Enemy attacked at 10 p.m. Intense musketry. C & D Companies relieved by A & B at 5.15 p.m. Casualties 1 K and 1 wounded. A & B relieved at 8.30 a.m. by C & D Companies. Intermittent firing from snipers all day, and shelled from 4.30 – 6.30 p.m. Snipers disposed of by following at under parapet for protection against shell fire. Casualties 2 K & 4 wounded. A & B Coys relieved C & D at dawn. Shelling very bad today. At 11.70 a.m. the French on our right retired and left an art.y exposed. The two Coys in support came up and filled up the gap. Sustaining severe casualties in doing so. This line was held until 7.30 p.m. when the French reoccupied it assisted by our own Companies who occupied another 50 yds of frontage. Casualties:— Lt-Colonel D. WARREN } Killed Captain R.E. WILSON Lieut R.S. PRINGLE died of wounds in hospital. Lieut I. REMONDER wounded Capt C.F. Wilson DSO injured 26th All? Other ranks and assumed command. 6 Killed and 48 wounded. C and D relieve A and B Coys before dawn. Trenches further improved. Shelled from 6 am till 3.15 p.m. without a respite. Casualties not heavy except for one platoon where the trenches had not been deepened enough owing to lack of time. Casualties:— 2 Lieut E. D. Drew wounded 3 CO's and men 6 Killed, 48 wounded and 16 missing.	Type of trenches found most effective. [sketch of trench cross-section with measurements: +9", 3", 13", 2'6", 3'4", 2'1"] The Commanding Officer and Captain Wilson were buried in PAISSY Church Yard.

WAR DIARY
or
INTELLIGENCE SUMMARY.

(Erase heading not required.)

Army Form C. 2118.

Instructions regarding War Diaries and Intelligence Summaries are contained in F.S. Regs., Part II. and the Staff Manual respectively. Title pages will be prepared in manuscript.

Hour, Date, Place	Summary of Events and Information	Remarks and references to Appendices
PAISSY RIDGE. 19th Sept.	Enemy attacked at 1 a.m. a blinding rain storm between repulsed. Relieved by COLDSTREAM GUARDS at 3 a.m. and Battn marched to VENDRESSE where we went into bivouac. We now formed an own Bdn and were acting in support to the WELCH REGT. Casualties - Nil.	
VENDRESSE. 20th Sept.	Reinforced the 1st R. Bde with 2 Companies at 2 p.m. to reinforce in support on the SHERWOOD FORESTERS had recaptured the Trenches vacated by the WEST YORKSHIRE REGT. At 5.6 p.m. returned to C.O.D. at 10.15 p.m. Lieut ROSE TROUPE and Lieut POUND joined with 197 2nd COS and men (3rd Reinforcement.) Casualties - Nil.	
21st Sept.	A & D relieved by C & B at 5.30 a.m. and later remained all day in reserve to the 1st & 2nd Bde. Major H.C. PILLEAU DSO died of wounds in hospital at NEUILLY.	
22nd Sept.	A & C relieved C.O.D. at 6.30 a.m. Alarm at 11 a.m. whole Battn reinforced 1st E Bde and remained in reserve. The 3rd R. Bde replaced 1st R. Bde in the trenches at 6 p.m. Our own Bdn 9 shelled shot and caused 5 casualties. Total casualties Men 1 K and 9 wounded.	
23rd Sept.	Quiet day except snipers. Lieut BURTON joined Battn Casualties 5 wounded.	

WAR DIARY or INTELLIGENCE SUMMARY.

Army Form C. 2118.

Hour, Date, Place	Summary of Events and Information	Remarks and references to Appendices
Nr VENDRESSE Sept 24th Sept 25th	Quiet day except snipers. Casualties 1 K and 2 wounded. C. Col. shelled by our own Art'y being short. Casualties 2 killed and 5 wounded.	
Sept 26th	The enemy commenced an attack at 4 a.m. before it was light, and reached to within 100 yards or front at 200 yd range. The right of D Co. and left of C Co opened fire, also a m machine gun and inflicted heavy losses. Our Art'y again shortly after were responsible for nearly all casualties which were :— Lieut H.J.P. Thompson wounded. 3 3 C.O's and men killed and 20 wounded.	On this day there were over 50 dead counted in front of our trenches as a result of the above action.
Sept 27th	Shelled at 5.15 p.m. Enemy had burst range but no casualties. We moved trenches to good trenches. Relieved at 10 p.m. by 1st COLDSTREAM GUARDS, and marched to BOEUILLY with remainder of 3rd Bn. when we went into billets and acted as Corps reserve. Casualties 1 wounded.	
Sept 28th	Stood to arms 4.30 - 5.30 a.m. Rifle inspection. Company Letters etc. Casualties - 13 missing.	Sir Douglas Haig rode over to congratulate the Bn. on doing so well.
OEUILLY Sept 29th	Stood to arms 4.30 to 5.30. Cleaned up billets. Rifle inspection. Paraded at 11 a.m. to General LOMAX Comdg 1st Division. He said that during the retreat he had noticed our Batt'n in particular as being amongst the best marchers in the Division as regards discipline. He had often thought to himself that surely such a Batt'n would gain first on the R. AISNE and up on the ridges and the V.C. paid.	

WAR DIARY.

Copied from 1st page of
War Diary for October

OEUILLY

on the right had held their own for 5 days. If our Commanding Officer had lived he would have received a distinction. Captain C.F.WATSON D.S.O. was recommended for a Brevet and had now been granted the local rank of Major. He had been obliged to keep the 3rd Brigade upm in the firing line for 15 days though he had tried on two occasions to get them back for a rest.   Casualties - nil.

30th Sept.   Stood to arms 4.30 to 5.30 a.m. Battn. paraded under Company arrangements for Physical Training and rifle inspections.
Casualties -Nil.

Army Form C. 2118.

WAR DIARY of The Queen's Regt.
INTELLIGENCE SUMMARY 14th Sept to 19th Sept.
(Erase heading not required.)

Hour, Date, Place	Summary of Events and Information	Remarks and References to Appendices
14th Sept. PAISSY	Summary of situation on 14th Sept &c	
7.15 am	At 7:15 am 14th Sept, the Queen's left- PAISSY under orders to advance towards AILLES & to be responsible for the safety of the Artillery on the right of 2nd Bde. On arrival about the CHEMIN DES DAMES the Bn came under heavy fire (machine gun, rifle & guns) but advanced	
10.0 am	took LA BOVELLE FM.	
11.0 am	At 11 am owing to a retirement on the left (party of 2nd Bde) the Bn found itself getting surrounded & a retirement made at the same time the leading coys at close quarters (20 yards in places) although heavy casualties inflicted on the Germans, the Bn failed to establish its officers killed & wounded & a large number of men.	
2 pm	The Bn was now 140 o.r. in front of the guns & in view of the fact that troops on the right & left were on the CHEMIN DES DAMES the C.O. decided to retire to that line at 2 pm which was successfully carried out, & touch joined with the French on our right. Bn held its position, 2 Coys in trenches, 2 Co in support.	
15th & 16th Sept		
17th Sept	About noon the Germans after continuous shell fire, made a determined attack on our position, our own & the French gave way leaving our Artillery exposed. Two (Cont.)	[A point is made of the situations on 14th & 17th Sept, as the Bn was almost isolated, being torn from its own Brigade]

Army Form C. 2118.

Queens Regt

WAR DIARY
or
INTELLIGENCE SUMMARY (Sheet 2)
(Erase heading not required.)

Instructions regarding War Diaries and Intelligence Summaries are contained in F. S. Regs, Part II. and the Staff Manual respectively. Title pages will be prepared in manuscript.

Hour, Date, Place	Summary of Events and Information	Remarks and References to Appendices
17th Sept 1pm CHEMIN DES DAMES	Companies in reserve advanced through the retiring Zouaves under very heavy fire & drove back the Germans. The Artillery were then able to reoccupy the position. The situation at the time was extremely critical. The men behaved splendidly. The Colonel (Warren) & the Adjutant were killed about this time, another officer wounded, 6 men killed 46 wounded. The German Artillery fire too extremely heavy shrapnel along the trenches. During the afternoon several small attacks were made but successfully driven off.	
18th Sept 19th Sept	Bn under heavy shell fire all day (70 casualties) relieved at 3 AM by the Coldstream Guards.	

BATTLE OF THE AISNE

14th September

REPORT BY THE QUEEN'S REGIMENT

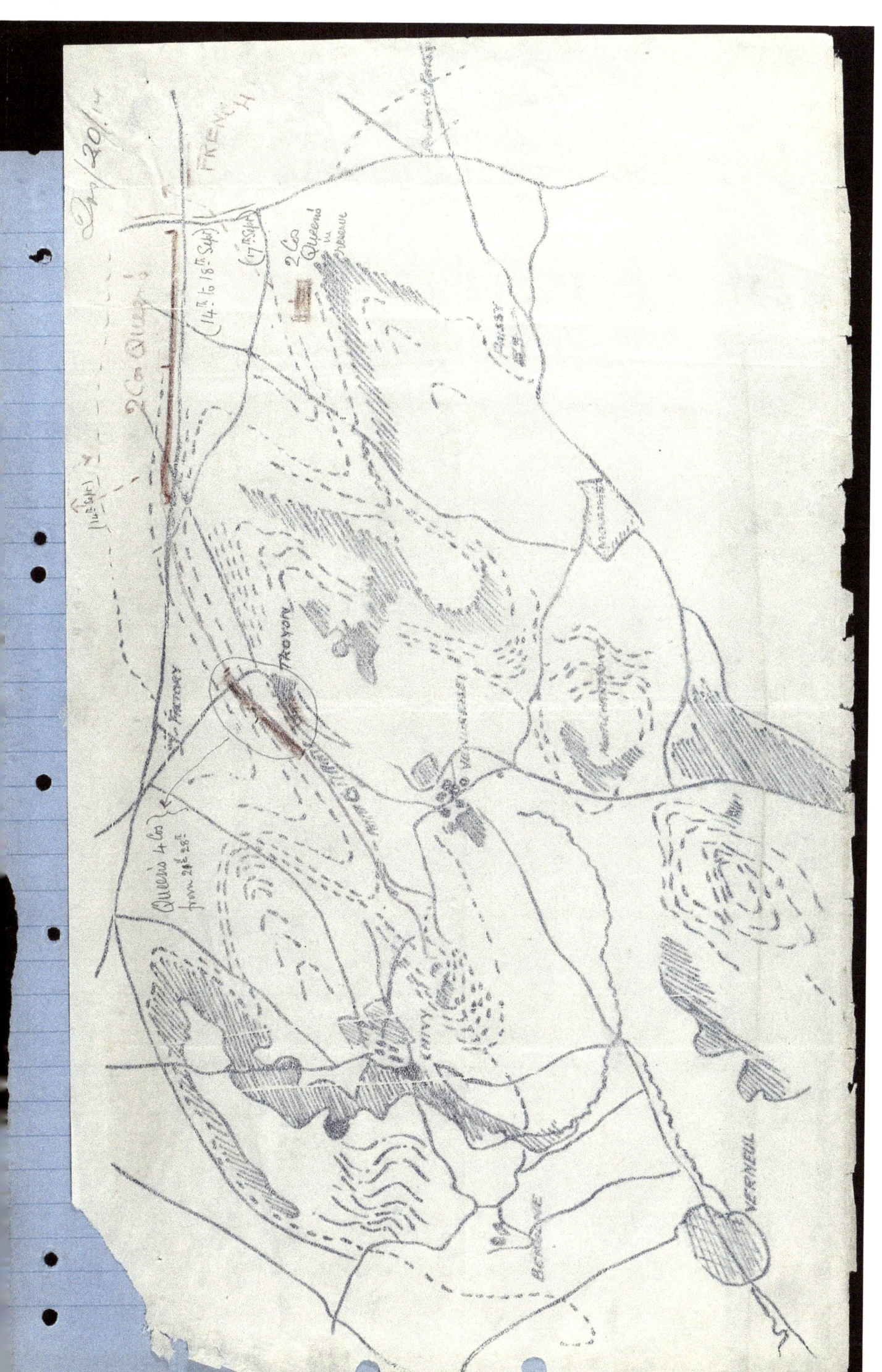

"A" Form.   Army Form C. 2121.
MESSAGES AND SIGNALS.
No of Message _____

Prefix ____ Code ____ m.	Words	Charge	This message is on a/c of :	Recd. at ____ m.
Office of Origin and Service Instructions	Sent			Date ____
	At ____ m.		Service	From ____
	To			
	By		(Signature of "Franking Officer.")	By ____

TO   All Bde Queen

| Sender's Number | Day of Month | In reply to Number | |
| * | 28 | | AAA |

Following from 1st Div. — Herewith 4 rough tracings of our position & general line of trenches held. I shall be very much obliged if you can collect any data from units regarding the following points — Original direction of their attack on 14th Sept — Furthest point reached & general direction in which it was facing at that time, and time of its withdrawal. The above information is required for historical records. Rough sketch of VERNAY by units which reached that place and a brief account of the fighting round that place and the pottery would be most useful if submitted, after revision by you. Information asked for submitted through H Qrs together with a plan as soon as possible

From 3rd Bde
Place Cuinchy
Time 2.18 pm

3rd Bde   Herewith —

The above may be forwarded as now corrected.   (Z)

Censor.   Signature of Addressor or person authorised to telegraph in his name

*This line should be erased if not required

3rd Brigade.

1st Division.

1st BATTALION

THE QUEEN'S ROYAL WEST SURREY REGIMENT

OCTOBER 1 9 1 4

Appendices attached:-

    1 to 15. - Report on Operations GHELUVELT.
                 Situation Reports.
                 Sketch Maps
                 Map ROULERS.

1st Division
3rd Inf.Bde.

WAR DIARY

(QUEEN'S) 1st Bn. The R.WEST SURREY REGT.

OCTOBER

1 9 1 4

Report on Operation at ~~GHELUVE~~ GHELUVELT
October 30/31st.

War Diary.

Appendices I to XIV.

Appx 15

Report on Fighting
Oct 30ᵗʰ – Nov 2ⁿᵈ 1914

app. XV

Report on fighting Oct 30 - Nov 2

On Oct 30ᵗʰ the 1ˢᵗ Bⁿ The Queen's held a line of entrenchments from the MENIN road near B 8 SE of GHELUVELT exclusive, across the three roads leading S from GHELUVELT as far as the stream by L 21.d. This line included two farms at L 22 a and was held by 4 Coys of Queen's. During night 30/31ˢᵗ two companies 3/K.R.R. came up as a support and one Coy was put in the front line and one in support.

Just about 7 pm 30ᵗʰ an attack was made on farm at top of 2 of fig 22 and repulsed, sniping took place throughout the night 30/31, and just before dawn 31ˢᵗ an attack was made on the two farms but again repulsed, but the enemy occupied the trenches 300ˣ to our front vacated by 22ⁿᵈ Bde and dug fresh trenches to the South. About 7 am a systematic bombardment of our section of defence commenced from two sides & continued throughout the morning. A platoon of 2/K.R.R in an advanced post in an orchard in L 22 C (where brown road goes) supported by one d/Queen's evacuated the trenches. W'd a counterattack by 60ᵗʰ was beaten back & the Enemy were enabled to hold on to the Orchard & work up 2 machineguns to within 200 yds of our trenches & to enfilade B B Co. About 11 am this company had to give way as they were also enfiladed from their left flank. The Germans had by this time set the farm

(2)
on fire and their bombardment was extremely heavy and accurate. At the same time a hostile infantry advance took place supported by several machine guns & our men were driven from their trenches by a heavy enfilade fire. From the left I received a report about this time that the Welch had evacuated their trenches & that our left Coy (D. Capt Creek's) was enfiladed. I next saw them being surrounded by Germans about 11.15 am.

Lt Boyd & myself left the farm L 22 C as the Germans entered it & tried to collect what men we could to rally on, but from the rising ground S. of N° 55 I saw the left Coy surrounded & Germans pushing into CHELUVELT behind us. I ordered what men I could to reform behind the 60th Rifles & L. N. Lancashire Regt. but these Regts were in their turn enfiladed by machine guns from CHELUVELT & retired back together. If the left had only stood firm I have no doubt that ½ of the Bn could have been collected. Col PELL DSO. was hit & had his leg broken, he was placed in a cavern in the farm yard with our medical Officer, as it was found impossible owing to the shell fire to take him away, & when the farm was rushed he was captured.

That evening we collected about 20 men and put them in the trenches of the Welch Regt.

(3) Eventually about 40 men were collected all that remained.

Sergt Major ELLIOT did very good service in taking messages under heavy fire and arranging for ammunition supply.

Lieut J. A. Boyd also behaved splendidly in an extremely trying situation.

Lt Boyd & myself were the only officers who got away.

           G F Watson Capt & Maj
6 Nov 1914   Comdg 1/Queen's

Army Form C. 2118.

WAR DIARY
or
INTELLIGENCE SUMMARY.
(Erase heading not required.)

Instructions regarding War Diaries and Intelligence Summaries are contained in F.S. Regs., Part II. and the Staff Manual respectively. Title pages will be prepared in manuscript.

Hour, Date, Place	Summary of Events and Information	Remarks and references to Appendices
OEUILLY.	On the night was held the air for 3 days. If an commanding officer had tried he could have received a lot children. Captain C.F. Luxton D.S.O. in command for 3 days, and had now been granted the leave and 4 days he had been obliged to keep the 3rd/4th up in the firing line for 5 days though he had tried on two occasions to get them back for a rest. Casualties - Nil.	
30th Sept.	9.30 to 11.am. Batt: paraded under Company Arrangements for Physical Training and Rifle Inspection. Casualties - Nil.	(1) KINGS REGT. (2) A n 8 & 6th QUEENS REGT. (3) c n D - (4) WELSH REGT. Dispositions — N. From Verneuil
1st October.	Stood to arms 4.30 to 5.30 a.m. Church Parade (Voluntary) at 9 a.m. Left Neufchat 6.30 p.m. and marched to VERNEUIL. B + D Coys relieved the 6th & Rifles in Trenches & A + C Coys remained in billets in the village as support. The KING'S Regt on our Left and WELSH REGT on our right. Of remaining Bdy, the J.W. Division was attached to the GUARDS BDE at VENDRESSE, and the GLOUCESTER REGT were at MOULINS. Enemy's nearest trenches are 300 yds in front. Casualties - nil.	
VERNEUIL. Oct 2nd	Quiet day except for snipers. Improved trenches considerably and concealed roadway to firing line. A + C Coys relieved B + D at 7 p.m. Casualties 3 wounded.	
Oct 3rd	Stood to arms from 4.30 to 5.30 in village. Transport conveyed four aeroplanes and took out iron pots with whistle. Colonel B.T. PELL D.S.O. joined the battln at 6 p.m. and assumed command. Attacked at 10 p.m. by enemy reported. Casualties 2 killed and 3 wounded.	

Forms/C. 2118/10

WAR DIARY
or
INTELLIGENCE SUMMARY.
(Erase heading not required.)

Army Form C. 2118.

Instructions regarding War Diaries and Intelligence Summaries are contained in F. S. Regs., Part II. and the Staff Manual respectively. Title pages will be prepared in manuscript.

Hour, Date, Place	Summary of Events and Information	Remarks and references to Appendices
VERNEUIL Oct 4th Oct 5th	Another day except snipers. Casualties 4 wounded.	
Oct 6th	A good deal of shelling in the village. Enemy seen constructing wire entanglements in front of trenches and fired on. Casualties 3 wounded.	
Oct 7th	Snipers had today, and a good deal of shelling. Casualties 1 killed and 7 wounded.	
Oct 8th	Shelled at intervals all day in the village. Casualties 1 killed and 8 wounded.	
	Quiet day. 10 officers and 39 men joined Batt'n at 1 a.m. on Oct 9th (4th Reinforcement). Names of officers as follows:— Capt BARTON, THORNEYCROFT and HODGSON. Lieuts. TANQUERAY, J.R. HAYES, LE BAS, HUNT, GREEN, WILLIAMS and SCHUNCK.	
Oct 9th	From 2 a.m. to 5.30 a.m. VERRY lights supplied to trenches into 3 reserve per Batt'n to fire them with. The enemy sniping badly in their trenches tonight, probably because ANTWERP had fallen. A few of enemy was seen to be placing wire entanglements in front and were fired on. Casualties 1 killed and 6 wounded.	These lights were found to be of great use. Attacks on the few occasions on which they were needed.
Oct 10th	Quiet day. Casualties 1 killed.	

Army Form C. 2118.

WAR DIARY
or
INTELLIGENCE SUMMARY.
(Erase heading not required.)

Instructions regarding War Diaries and Intelligence Summaries are contained in F. S. Regs., Part II. and the Staff Manual respectively. Title pages will be prepared in manuscript.

Hour, Date, Place	Summary of Events and Information	Remarks and references to Appendices
VERNEUIL Oct 11th	A commanding position, covering the village was reconnoitred and strengthened for the supporting companies to occupy in case of need. The R.E. strengthened the wire entanglements in front of trenches.	Just so
Oct 12th	Quiet day till 11 p.m. Alarm in village and stood to arms. Heavy attack on VENDRESSE RIDGE was repulsed and our support not required. Casualties - Nil. Capt F.C. LONGBOURNE wounded.	
Oct 13th	Stood to arms in culler trench ready to support shelling. Casualties Captain M.V. FOY killed	
Oct 14th	Quiet day until after what had been counted out. Heavy firing on our right from WELCH REGT. and enemy's search-light turned on our trenches. All trenches relieved and collected at 1 a.m on 15th. One man killed Casualties - Nil.	
Oct 15th	All spare ammunition and rpts. collected and returned. Returned by French at 1.15 a.m 16th and C. & A. Companies regained H.Qrs at VERNEUIL. Companies marched independently through PONT ARCY, VIEIL ARCY, and VAUXIN to COURCELLES arrived here at about 7.0 a.m. Remained in billets and was in cover from aeroplanes all day. Casualties- Nil.	
COURCELLES Oct 16th 2.15 A.M.	Marched [A & B Coy] independently at 1.15 a.m and left at 1.15 a.m to LA FERE STA. Entrained at 11.15 a.m. Destination unknown	
On the move. Oct 17th	Passed LA FERTE MILON, VILLERS, ORMOZ, NANTOY, DAMMARTIN, Reached PARIS at 4.0 a.m. Destination still unknown.	

WAR DIARY
or
INTELLIGENCE SUMMARY.
(Erase heading not required.)

Army Form C. 2118.

Hour, Date, Place	Summary of Events and Information	Remarks and references to Appendices
HONDEGHEM. Oct 18.	Pared EPLUCHES, ETAPLE, ST POL. One Platoon 1/A Coy fully dressed and equipped all night in case of alarm. CALONNE at 8.30 a.m. CHOQUES at 9/15 a.m. Back roll through LILLERS, HAZEBROUCK at 10.30 a.m. and entrained at CASSEL. Marched to HONDEGHEM and went into billets. Posted outposts and sentries on billets.	See Map "ROOLERS" No 20
Oct 19. On the move Oct 20.	Rest day. Nothing concerned. Casualties - Nil. The Batt: marched off at 5.30 A.M. through SILVESTRE, STEENVOORDE, L'ABEELE and POPERINGHE and went into billets in scattered farms just W of ELVERDINGHE. Companies found their own protection.	
On the move Oct 21st	The Batt: moved out into the main road at 2 a.m. and assembled in the nbr B.M.C.D. The 7/N St army advanced from today to the Division and Our Batt: leaving the 2oth, pushed through ELVERDINGHE, BOESINGHE and LANGEMARCK. The Batt: deployed on the N.E. of the latter village. Objective:- To make good line of road running N.W. & S.E. through POELCAPELLE STA. (OSTEND MAR) B.& A Companies occupied frontage from road to railway with 2 platoons of A Coy on Northern flank of railroad. C & D Companies in support. As the firing line advanced we came under heavy fire from (1) as well as own friendly fire at (5). Companies extended at (4) and (3). D Coy now pushed forward to (5). At 1PM At this time also the 2 W. Border Regt made an attack to A Coy advanced to (2). on the right flank of the Batt: which was unsuccessful and they fell back exposing the right flank of B Coy. Capt HUNTER though found it necessary to drop back his Company though a messenger order, the remainder of B Coy fell back and a interim was made to c.b.c. M&C as they were doing at A Coy and D were now obliged to withdraw in consequence and considerable	(1) B Coy. Enemy Position (2) B Coy 1/Queens (3) D & A Coy 1/Queens (later 2 platoons) (4) D Coy and 2 Platoons 1/A Coy 1/Queens (5) C Coy 1/Queens

Army Form C. 2118.

WAR DIARY
or
INTELLIGENCE SUMMARY.
(Erase heading not required.)

Instructions regarding War Diaries and Intelligence Summaries are contained in F.S. Regs., Part II. and the Staff Manual respectively. Title pages will be prepared in manuscript.

Hour, Date, Place	Summary of Events and Information	Remarks and references to Appendices
400° S.W. of LANGEMARCK. Oct 22nd	Losses were suffered during this short Advance. A Trick line was occupied and entrenched when the supporting Company was located and no further advance was met with. Relieved by WELCH REGT 3.0 P.M. Casualties:— Captain THORNEYCROFT wounded and missing Lieut POUND wounded 2 Lieut LE BAS wounded 127 C.O's & men killed, 68 wounded and 8 missing. The Batt. started to Turnout into the S.W. of LANGEMARCK. The Batt. entrenched at 3.30 a.m. facing N.W. and on a S. side of railway. At 3 p.m. C. & D Cos were attacked N of railway and then fell back supporting C. then the further supports shook the Trenches. At 7 p.m. C Co was sent off as escort to Artillery and A Co broken up to C & D's trenches At 11.30 p.m. A.B & Co's went to (5) where a first line was entrenched during the night facing North. Casualties 2 killed and 2 wounded.	[map sketch with LANGEMARCK STA., N arrow, numbered points ①②③④⑤]
Oct 23rd	At 11.30 a.m. the Batt. was ordered to attack the INN. About 1000 yds N of an Junction EAST (OSTEND MAP) A Co in front, D Co in support. Despatched B Co & D Co to WEST. The advance was accomplished without much loss & within 70 yds of the INN, a fusor of D Co was thrown into front trench, captured about 60 prisoners, 4 men of the 2nd CAMERON HIGHLANDERS and captured the INN. D Co then advanced through N of LINLANGS. LINLANGS BIXSCHOOTE - LANGEMARCK supported by A & B Companies to the left rear and right rear, and the left flank of D Company 2 Coys of Camerons (with Captn Gregory Lt Franks as the cavalry at instructed reported attacks and could command were in Khaki and they were unable to retire to to an advance Gregory, Capt Franks, Lt Greaves in Khaki had wished then was a part. The Batt occupied the main trench the night and entrenched until dawn & to relieve D during the night and there were no left of B and D Companies replaced C by an escort of Arty.	[map sketch showing L.N.L. positions, Northampton, Queen's INN, Carnarvon, German attack arrow 6 p.m.] Capt Crerar got D.S.O for his work Capt A.D Coyon. This diary, ???

Forms/C. 2118/10

WAR DIARY
or
INTELLIGENCE SUMMARY.
(Erase heading not required.)

Army Form C. 2118.

Hour, Date, Place	Summary of Events and Information	Remarks and references to Appendices
Oct 23rd 10.30 am	The Bn. was holding trenches in Square EE 9(a) under a little shell fire which commenced about 9 am. At 10.30 orders came from 2nd / Bde (Gen BULFIN) to retake the "INN" (X 23 c) and close the "gap" between the Northamptons & Camerons. Events proved there was no "gap" —	Map "ROULERS" No 20 – App. I. Map (A)
	At 11.15 am the B" advanced A Coy on E of main road, D Coy (Capt Cresh) on W with B Co. (Capt Hunter) in support. The advance of 600 yds was made under considerable hostile artillery fire, but D Coy got 6" down to the line of the Camerons about 70 yds from the "INN". Sgt MONK's platoon rushed the Inn supported by a Company & captured about 60 Germans & released some 50 Cameron prisoners.	
Noon	About noon Major WATSON organized a general advance of the line including about 2 Coys Camerons & part of L.N. Lancs. Capt Cresh advanced on the right & soon the whole line went forward capturing about 200 Germans & a lot of wounded. Orders were then received re-occupy the "old line of trenches" N of the main road. D Co did so, but the Northamptons line rept on our right did not arrive. Thus D Co's flank was rather exposed. The enemy kept up sniping all day, not some horse arn fire on the main road about bit.Inn. made an attack on D Co's right flank. They roughly up & riddled Cresh's trench 2 machine guns and	see sketch – Appendix II

Army Form C. 2118.

WAR DIARY
or
INTELLIGENCE SUMMARY.
(Erase heading not required.)

Instructions regarding War Diaries and Intelligence Summaries are contained in F. S. Regs., Part II. and the Staff Manual respectively. Title pages will be prepared in manuscript.

Hour, Date, Place	Summary of Events and Information	Remarks and references to Appendices
Oct 23 1914 6.30 pm	A Co was in support but could not fire as the enemy were between them and D Co. The enemy captured part of the trenches and Capt Crick brought the remainder of his men out by advancing round (the enemy) right flank in the confusion. Some of the enemy were dressed in khaki on this occasion. The supporting line held on and checked the enemy — reinforcements were sent up by 2nd Bn. but were not required. C Coy relieved D Coy and D Coy with remainder of B Co went as escort to guns and to Bn H.Q respectively. B Co of this day were used indubitably to reinforce parts of the line as required from some got captured with part of C Coy. Casualties:— Capt Hawk ") "Lt William" slightly wounded Capt Hodgson Speed " killed 10 O Co's men killed 35 wounded and 89 missing.	Capt Crick received a D.S.O for this action.

WAR DIARY or INTELLIGENCE SUMMARY

Army Form C. 2118.

Hour, Date, Place	Summary of Events and Information	Remarks and references to Appendices

In Trenches. Oct 24th

Casualties:—
Capt. HUNTER and 2/Lieut. B. HAYES wounded.
Capt. HOBSON injured by fall.
16 2 Co's men killed, 33 wounded, and 23 missing.

Quiet night. Shelled during the day. Enemy attacked at 6.30 and 8.30 pm. was repulsed. Fresh relieved on 2 Companies at 11 p.m. 15 men of a time. The quarters were carried out successfully, within 100 y[ar]ds of the enemy's advanced trenches. The unexpired turns in our men, from enemy's advanced trenches. The Batt. reassembled in the wood E of PILCEM, casualties sustained. The Batt. marched during the night to HOOGE. Casualties — Nil.
— The Batt. marched during the night to HOOGE. Casualties — Nil.

HOOGE. Oct 25.

Rest day. Capt. SOAMES & WOOD joined with 40 men. (5th Reinforcement)

Oct 26—

The Batt. moved into wood at BELLEWAARDE FARM until 11 p.m. then into VELDHOEK WOOD on N of main road. Bivouacked there for the night.

Oct 27—

The Batt. was in reserve till 3 P.M. today and entrenched in the wood N of E ZANDVOORDE. Retired at 11 p.m. to Bivouac immediately in front leading to BELLEWAARDE FARM. Casualties — Nil.

Oct 28—

Quiet day and Batt. remained in Bivouac.

IN TRENCHES E. OF GHELUVELT. Oct 29th

Capt. ALDWORTH joined the Batt. with 95 9 Co's men. (6th Reinforcement) The attack continued. The 22nd Bde attacked in conjunction at 5.30a.m. All companies were attacked — around BCo attacked at dawn to a look out occupied by our 2nd Batt. with cooperate S.E of GHELUVELT. The line was subsequently at 11pm and police was given for a permanent line to be taken up about 6.00 am E of GHELUVELT facing EAST.

WAR DIARY or INTELLIGENCE SUMMARY

Army Form C. 2118.

Hour, Date, Place	Summary of Events and Information	Remarks and references to Appendices
Oct 29th 1914	The 22nd Bde held a line from about 1½ kilos E of GHELUVELT (K22 6.) to KRUISEEKE (S 3 a) Those westward towards ZANDVOORDE. News was received that this line had been penetrated N party of 3rd Bde was ordered to reinforce this line. The WELCH & 2nd to took the N of MENIN road.	
10 AM	About 10 a.m. the Batn arrived at GHELUVELT & proceeded to support the 2nd Bn Queen's about 1 kil SE of the village (K22 a), who held the line out to KRUISEEKE. In approximately as shown on the sketch, three was a German trench in front of "C" & "B" by which A Coy were ordered to take about 3 p.m. An advance was made but the company could not take the trench in spite of assistance on its right flank by some companies of "Gnats". They were pillowed a merein, & were withdrawn at dusk.	Ref. app. III Sketch B Ref. app III
3pm		
11pm	At 11 p.m. the 1st Bn. occupied the line as shown on the sketch with 22nd Bde still in front. This Bde received orders to contract their line and escape to our right – Ft Egstoood was Kelly & Lt. Beecham wounded this day.	Ref. app I & II
Oct 30.	This morning 7 30 O.R. was occupied in withdrawing the 22nd Bde. chiefly 2/Queens, from our front, and besides some shelling there was little change. Two Corp K.R.R. came up to support the Bn during the evening & entrenched round farm ①.	Ref. app VII Ref. app VIII Ref. app IX

WAR DIARY
or
INTELLIGENCE SUMMARY.
(Erase heading not required.)

Army Form C. 2118.

Hour, Date, Place	Summary of Events and Information	Remarks and references to Appendices
GHELUVELT 31st Oct 1914 7am 11 am	At 7pm an attack on C Coy was repulsed — Before dawn an attack was made on C, B & the KRR, but was repulsed. The enemy dug-in within 300ʸ of our lines & vacated the trenches vacated by 9/10th. At 7am our line had subjected to a very heavy bombardment which our guns were unable to reply to. The enemy worked their bay into the redout at ③ & the platoon of K.R.R. supported by 1 platoon Queen's under Lt Tanqueray were driven out. Col Pell 890. ordered a counterattack but the attempt by the KRR failed. Thus the enemy got the redout within 150 y of our line. Major Watson went back for assistance but none was available & he then returned to find Col Pell wounded. The command came in & we were holding our own when B Coy about 10am. were driven out of their trenches by ew. shire gun fire from both flanks. & the Queens (2 platoons KRR) were sent for, but could not be found. It is believed they moved towards D Co without orders. Soon after this Capt Creek sent a message saying that he had heard the Welch had succeeded their trenches but he was quite alright & would hold on. Major Watson went to A Coy to arrange a counterattack in the West of the Enemy coming in from ①. He himself moved up to the ridge to see how the left was getting on. When there he met a	Ref App X Ref App XI Ref App XII Ref App. XIII & XIV

Army Form C. 2118.

WAR DIARY
or
INTELLIGENCE SUMMARY.
(Erase heading not required.)

Instructions regarding War Diaries and Intelligence Summaries are contained in F. S. Regs., Part II. and the Staff Manual respectively. Title pages will be prepared in manuscript.

Hour, Date, Place	Summary of Events and Information	Remarks and references to Appendices
	A word was sent from D Coy. that situation then appeared that the Germans about C Coy trenches (no doubt could be got from this Coy) B Coy trenches evacuated, were retiring from farm ⒶA with the Germans entering it. Orders were sent to D Coy to retire but before the order arrived the Germans were seen in the village behind D Coy.* Major Watson & Lt. Boyd then reformed what men they could about the house at Ⓐ and the few men of the K.R.R. went back to rally on their Pon. As the Germans were now in the village the above rally if hastily moved towards the K.R.R.	It afterwards appeared that soon soon after Major Watson left the farm, that the Germans entered it. * This orderly came back & said that the Germans were surrounding them.
11.30 am	who were then actually moving back, owing it is said to a report that hostile machine guns were bringing up to enfilade them. There was thus nothing closer to rally on. Major Watson & Lt. Boyd then rallied men of different regiments & put them into trenches in K 20(b). The Guards of 2nd Divⁿ reoccupied GHELOVELT during the afternoon but the line of trenches was reconstructed on the W side of the village. About 20 men only were collected & the remainder were either wounded or missing.	1 Machine gun } captured. 1 S.A.A Cart } 2 tools each

ROULERS

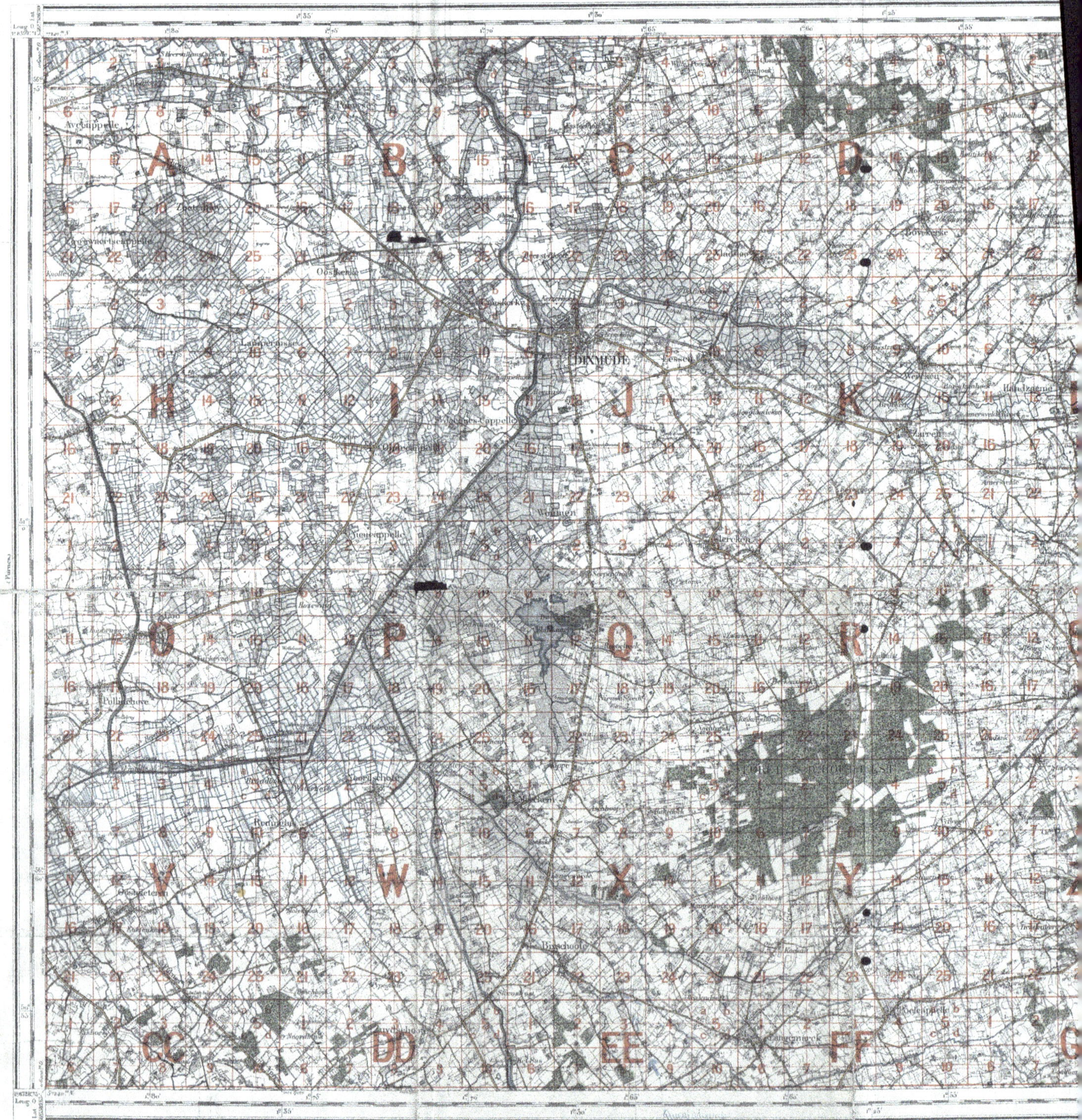

Geographical Section General Staff, No. 2743.

NOTE.

The map is divided into large squares, lettered "A," "B," "C," "D," etc., the sides of which are 6,000 yards in length.

The large squares are divided into 25 smaller squares, numbered 1 to 25, the sides of which are 1,000 yards in length.

The areas 6, 7, 8, 9, 10, in squares CC, DD, EE, FF, GG, HH, JJ, are rectangles of 1,000 yards by 530 yards.

The minor squares and rectangles are to be considered as lettered "a," "b," "c," "d," but the letters are only printed in one small square in each large square to avoid confusing the map.

A point can thus be described as lying in square A.2.c., D.5.a., etc.

If the position of a point can be identified more closely, the further description N, S, E, or W may be added.

If only the description of the small squares is given, e.g. A.2., the position indicated will be taken to be the centre of A.2. Similarly, A.2.d. will be taken as meaning the centre of the minor square A.2.d. unless a further description N., S., etc., is added.

The description A.2.c.d. can be used if uncertainty exists as to whether "c" or "d" is the correct minor square.

Appendix I

ROULERS

20

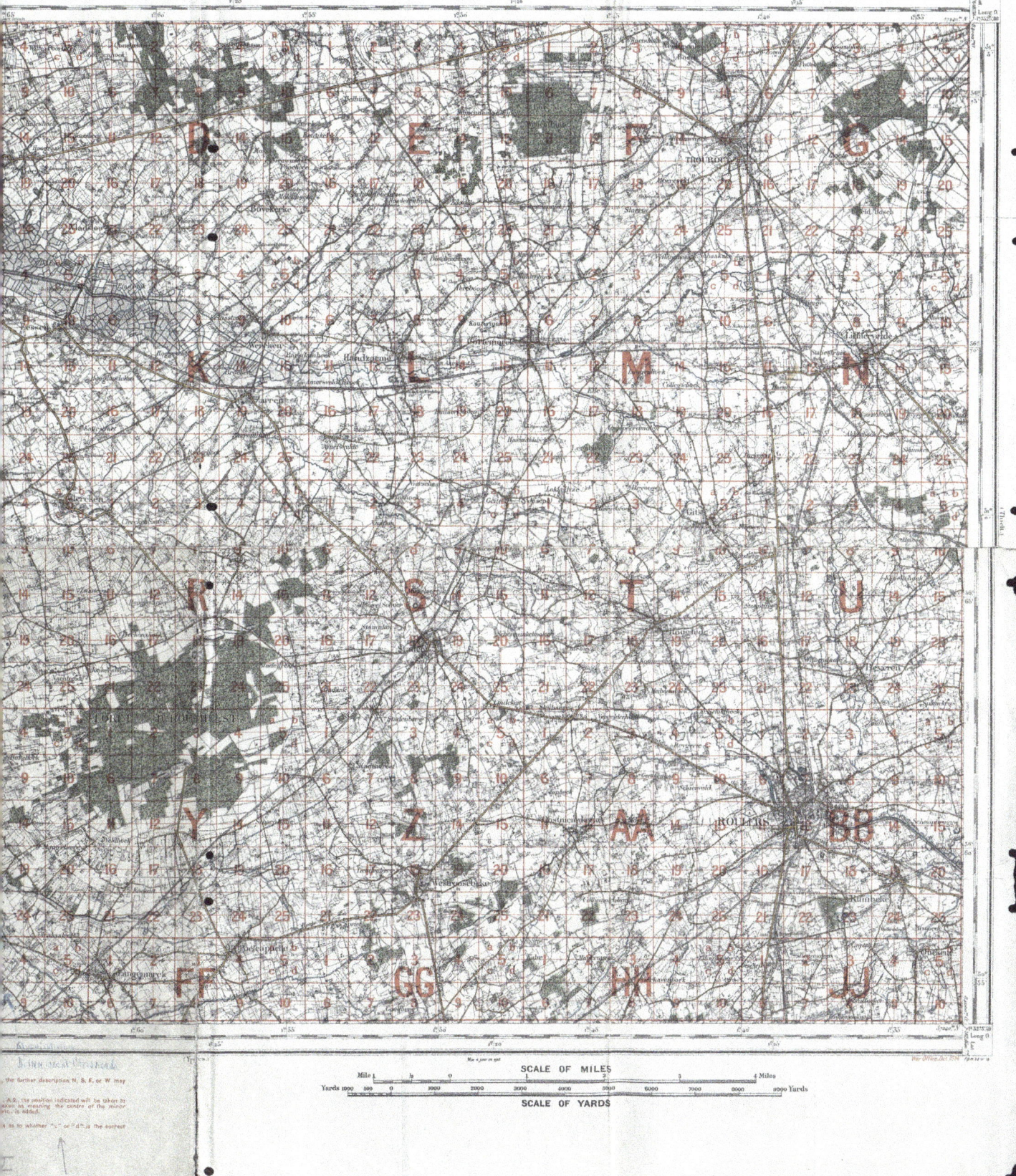

SCALE OF MILES
SCALE OF YARDS

ROULERS
(with Squares)

"A" Form. — MESSAGES AND SIGNALS. — Army Form C. 2121.

TO: 3rd Brigade

I think my leading Company is on road between GHELUVELT and ZANDVOORDE with its left close to village & I am not absolutely certain of the position of this Company. My Second Company is about 300x west of leading Company with left resting on village of GHELUVELT. My third Company practically prolongs the line of my Second Company. The fourth Company is about 400x in rear. I have received your message about concentration near P of POEZELHOEK and have sent it to Major WATSON who is with leading Company. I understand from your message that you do not want the troops on right of road to press forward until situation at POELZEHOEK has been cleared up. I have seen nothing of 7th Division who should I understand be on our right.

D.J. Colt Lt Colonel
O.C. 1/ Queens

Time: 1.15 am

Appx. II

APPENDIX II
SKETCH MAP of action on Oct 23rd 1914

German counterattack

From BIXSCHOOTE

L. N. Lancs.   Camerons   [N.H.]   A Co.   2 Coy Northamptons   hedges &c
                                                Other Coys   To LANGEMARCK

1 Co Northampton

D Coy   A Co (H. Bn aux)

D Coy   A & B Co Queens

To 2nd Bde. HQ   Bns HQ 22/23rd

Ⓐ

4-XII-14   C.F. Watson, 2nd Major
            2/Queens

20 Sec   20 East N23 – D17
          28 NE 3

Appx. III

"A" Form.   Army Form C. 2121.
MESSAGES AND SIGNALS.

Appendix III

TO: Queens Welch

Send Number: C   Day of Month: 2₉   AAA

Enemy appear to be massing on your left about Chateau near C J P20.C.4.0.6.5 1/40000 map. Guard Division are dealing with this AAA you should be careful about your left flank whilst pursuit is continued. NOM SWB are going to the left to support Scots Guards.

(2)

Major Watson

For your information it appears as if no further advance should be made on right of road until situation on left of road has been cleared up.

From: B/16th MGC
Time: 1 pm

Appx. IV

"A" Form.
MESSAGES AND SIGNALS.
Army Form C. 2121.

TO: Appendix IV
Queens

Sender's Number: 61
Day of Month: 29th
AAA

Push on as hard as you can and reoccupy trenches vacated this morning. A general forward movement is progressing along our line and the Germans are retiring on our left. Scots are clearing wood to [?] of GHELUVELT and [?] pushing on. Two battalions 2nd Bde on left are also being sent in to attack.

Place: Thicke [?]
Time: 1/35 pm

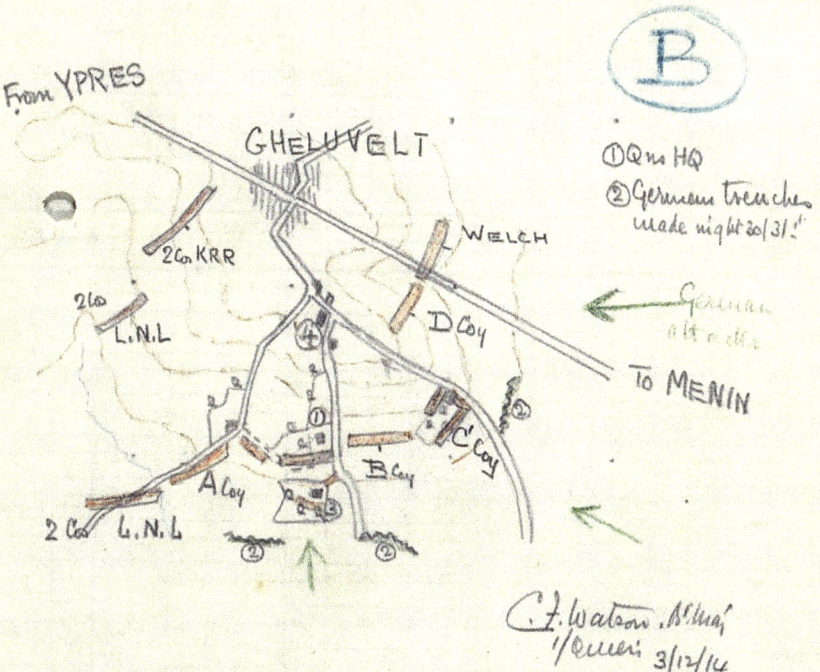

Appx VIII

"A" Form.   Army Form C. 2121.
MESSAGES AND SIGNALS.

Ref App VIII

Queens

Sender's Number	Day of Month	In reply to Number	
246	30th		AAA

A new line must be immediately established running from your right to the GHELUVELT - ZANDVOORDE road about 1 mile S of the VELDHOEK X roads AAA orders have been sent to you by Major Wilson and the situation explained to the Adjutant 2/ Queens who has just been here. The right of the 7th Division appears to have fallen back slightly but our Cavalry 3rd Bde was counter attacking Klein, and may relieve the situation. The 2nd Bde (less 2 Bns) was moving towards the wood where you were 3 days ago to support the 7th Div.

From
Place   1st Bde
Time   12/2 pm
                                (Z)
                                G. My

Appx VII

"A" Form.
MESSAGES AND SIGNALS.
Army Form C. 2121.

Prefix	Code	m.	Words	Charge		This message is on a/c of:	Recd. at _____ m.
Office of Origin and Service Instructions.			Sent				Date
			At _____ m.		Service.	From
			To App VII			By
			By		(Signature of "Franking Officer.")	

TO Queens
     SoB
     ?

* Sender's Number: 39
  Day of Month: 30
  In reply to Number:
  AAA

Situation does not permit change
suggestion. May 35th L. North
Lancs will hold line from right
of Queens to the point where the
stream crosses the GHELUVET —
ZANDVOORDE road. Seventh
Gunners will carry on line.

From
Place: WD 4
Time: 7/50 am
                          G ?

The above may be forwarded as now corrected. (Z)
Censor. Signature of Addressor or person authorised to telegraph in his name
*This line should be erased if not required.

appx IX

MESSAGES AND SIGNALS.

Army Form C. 2121.

To: App IX

TO 1st Queen's

Sender's Number: A22 Day of Month: 30-10-14

AAA

Your message received AAA find N.Lancs are uncertain of their ground AAA Please send me an officer or N.C.O. to guide their left and put it in touch with your right AAA. Am disappointed my companies cannot be returned, please inform G.O.C. 3rd Bde of their retention by you.

From: 2nd Rifles
Place:
Time:

appx X

Wt. W1154/9240 7/11. 7,500,000. Sch. 4a. "A" Form. Army Form C. 2121.
MESSAGES AND SIGNALS.

To: 1/ Queens

Sender's Number: 25 Day of Month: 30th

Germans are massing 300x in front of my trenches with fixed bayonets and I have informed my side that I do not intend to conform to suggested re-arrangement to night

From: Welch
Time: 7.7.15

Appx XI

"A" Form.
MESSAGES AND SIGNALS.
Army Form C. 2121.

TO: Queens

Sender's Number	Day of Month	In reply to Number	
1	31		AAA

Am endeavouring to get 21st Bde to prolong their line to stream crossing ZANDVOORDE – GHELUVELT road AAA if this is done you will hold line you held last night with Nind Lines on your right and you might then release KRR AAA Welch could not move their line owing to enemy in force just opposite them

From: 1st B dp

Time: 12/20 a.m.

G Bry

App. XII

"A" Form.
MESSAGES AND SIGNALS.

To: App XII

TO: Queens

Day of Month: 31st

I have just learnt that the L.N Lanc Regt are not in their right place and are pushed to their right about 900 yds beyond where they should be. aaa. I also understand that 2 Cos K.R.R. are filling up the gap that has occurred from this between your right & L.N. Lanc. AAA. Please let me know where your right is, and if you are satisfied you are not occupying too much front. ~~[struck through]~~ How many Cos have you in front line?

From: 3rd B de
Time: 3.15 am

Appx. XIII

Appendix XIII
To O.C. [illegible]

Enemy are entrenching about 300
to our front along the line of
farm buildings.
Could our artillery fire on them?
All right here.
                        [signature] Capt
                        Cmdg D Coy

10 a.m.

{ Please send more
{ ammunition

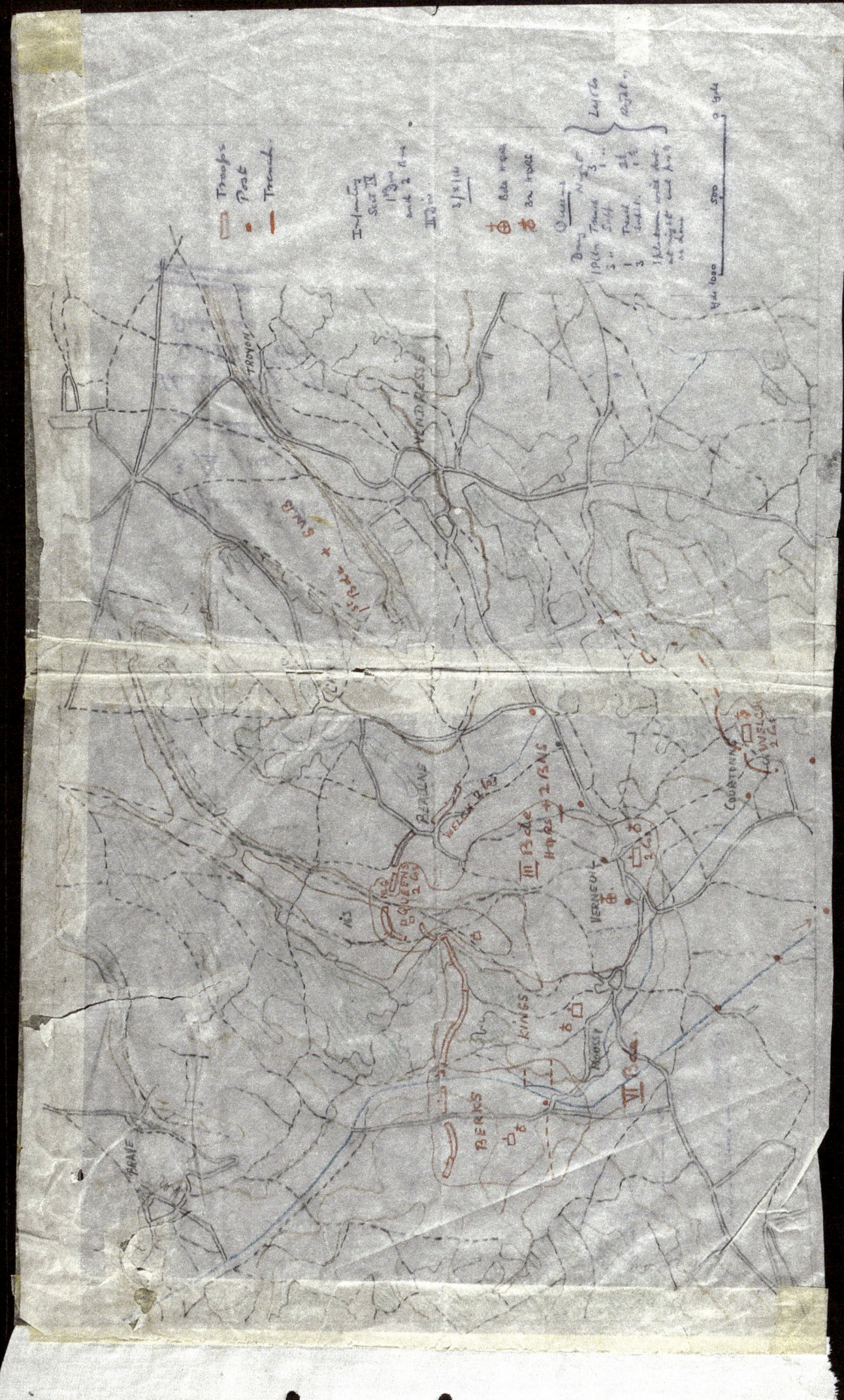

3rd Brigade.

1st Division.

Battalion became Corps Troops 8th November

1st BATTALION

THE QUEEN'S ROYAL WEST SURREY REGIMENT

NOVEMBER 1 9 1 4

1st Division
3rd Inf.Bde.

WAR DIARY

(QUEEN'S) 1st Bn. The R.WEST SURREY REGT.

NOVEMBER

1914

Battalion became Corps Troops 8/11/14.

Army Form C. 2118.

WAR DIARY
or
INTELLIGENCE SUMMARY.
(Erase heading not required.)

Hour, Date, Place	Summary of Events and Information	Remarks and references to Appendices
In trenches E of HOOGE. Nov. 1st	Casualties:- Lt.-Col PELL, Lieut TANQUERAY, and Captain SOAMES Wounded & Missing. Captains CREEK, BARTON, & ROSE (RAMC) missing. Lieutenants ROSE-TROUPE and GREEN missing. 124 2COs + men killed, wounded, & missing. Lieut TANQUERAY & CAPT WOOD wounded. Lieutenant BOYD collected about 200 stragglers of other Regiments and B Coy and augmented them in a line of trenches immediately E of HOOGE. Here the 1/Bn and 1m Am WELCH Fusiliers rejoined. 2nd Lieut FOWLER joined with 5 men from Hospital. The Batt = 432 men under Lieut BOYD reoccupied the 70th Rifles on the S side of HOOGE CHATEAU near GAGHELWELT and remained in support until dusk. Casualties 3 men wounded.	Ref APP XV (illegible) 1/2
Nov. 2nd	Major WATSON joined 3rd Batt Staff at 8 AM and Lieut BOYD took over Command of Batt. Remained in Trenches. Casualties killed and 3 wounded.	
Nov. 3rd	Quiet day. Batt. remained in Trenches.	
Nov. 4th	Major WATSON rejoined from 3rd Bde Hdqrs at 7 a.m. 2nd Lieut FOWLER went to WELCH REGT. as they were short of officers. Casualties. 2nd Lieut FOWLER.- wounded.	
BELLEWAARDE FARM Nov. 5th	Batt. retired to BELLEWAARDE FARM except 245 Regt who remained to support the Cavalry Regt which relieved us. Lt French S/of ZILLEBEKE.	(signature)
In trenches S of ZILLEBEKE Nov. 6th	Quiet day. 4 pm Bn turned into reinforce Lt French S/of ZILLEBEKE. WELCH REGT and 6th RIFLES advanced with the Gloucester Regt and Queens in support. Major WATSON left at 11pm to join Staff of 2nd Div? Casualties: 3rd	

Forms/C. 2118/10

WAR DIARY
or
INTELLIGENCE SUMMARY.
(Erase heading not required.)

Army Form C. 2118.

Hour, Date, Place	Summary of Events and Information	Remarks and references to Appendices
2 miles E. of ZILLEBEKE. Nov 7.	The QUEENS were sent up at 4.30 a.m. to reinforce the front line and dug in till dawn. The 22nd B.D.Coy advanced on our left to attack and reach from the line of the 2 WARTELEEN road which runs through Pt L of Reutel village. the GLOUCESTER REGT advanced to reinforce this line, & the 1st A.C. at 10 a.m. the Trenches until 9 p.m. when they received Trenches of the 9n occupied their Trenches. Entrenched all night and made one last own with drawn at morning. Casualties - nil	(YPRES MAP)
Nov 8th	Heavy firing at our trenches during the night at 10 a.m. at 4 a.m. but no attack. The Turks attacked our dawn towards HOLLEBEKE. The QUEENS were return to 10 p.m. by 6th Cav. Bde. The QUEENS were relieved to their to BRIEEN to 1st A.C. Hd Qrs. 49 ? C.O.s and men joined the Batt'n this evening (7th Reinforcement.)	
BRIELEN. Nov 9th	Batt'n organized into one Company (Letter A.) Total strength of Batt'n was 4. 2 Officers and 170 ? C.O.'s men (including attached)	
Nov 10th	Moved into hut billets. Day occupied in cleaning up billets etc.	
Nov 11th	Instructions to N.C.O.'s & great coats etc. 10 a.m. - 11 a.m. Battn rote parade of Rifle inspection	
Nov 12th	Parade 10.0 - 11.0 a.m. for Rifle Exam, great ditties etc.	
Nov 13th	Drill rota parade at 10.30 a.m. of instruction in great coats, rifle exercise etc. Strength of Batt'n including attached is 172 all ranks.	

Army Form C. 2118.

WAR DIARY
or
INTELLIGENCE SUMMARY.
(Erase heading not required.)

Hour, Date, Place	Summary of Events and Information	Remarks and references to Appendices
BRIELEN		
Nov 14th	All supplies brought up to the 1st Division.	
Nov 15th	Usual Routine — Snow fell today for the first time.	
Nov 16th	Usual Routine.	
Nov 17th	Usual Routine.	
Nov 18th	Usual Routine and Route march.	
Nov 19th	Usual Routine.	
Nov 20th	Captain R. Zeepham Duffield Regt joined the Battn and assumed command.	
Nov 21st	Paraded at 8.15 AM and marched via POPERINGHE and STEENVOORDE to HAZEBROUCK. Reached the latter at 6 PM. 2nd Lieut CHANDLER joined with 50 3COYs men (8th reinforcement)	
HAZEBROUCK		
Nov 22nd	Captain H.W. STENHOUSE, Captain PARNELL, Capt NEW (E Surrey Regt), Lieut PAIN, Lieut Thompson and 2nd Lieut VOISIN (E Surrey Regt) joined the Battn with 34 3COYs men (9th Reinforcement)	Lieut Doyle & Lt Airbuckle left for England on 10 days leave

Army Form C. 2118.

WAR DIARY
or
INTELLIGENCE SUMMARY.
(Erase heading not required.)

Instructions regarding War Diaries and Intelligence Summaries are contained in F. S. Regs., Part II. and the Staff Manual respectively. Title pages will be prepared in manuscript.

Hour, Date, Place	Summary of Events and Information	Remarks and references to Appendices
HAZEBROUCK.		
Nov 23rd 24th & 25th	Captain STENHOUSE assumed command of Battalion. Ordinary routine in billets.	
Nov 26th	Lieut Colonel H. Ste Wilkins from 1st Batt'n and assumed command.	
Nov 27th to 30th	Ordinary Routine	

Copy.   Letter from Capt. J.D. Boyd, D.S.O.,
                    1/The Queen's Royal Regiment,
                        Tournay Barracks, Aldershot.
                            2nd March 1923.

Dear Edmonds,

In reply to your letter of the 28th February, the first draft after 31st October, which joined us on 9th November, was a good one, consisting of reservists almost entirely. After that we fell off sadly in quality as well as quantity. The 2nd Battalion was also short of personnel and was filled up prior to the 1st Battalion owing to the latter being in corps troops.

It was only in January 1915 that a C Company could be formed from a draft which joined the battalion at Hinges. D Company was formed about February 1915. The men who joined us in January-February were very untrained and any sprinkling of trained N.C.O's and men amongst them were mostly medically unfit.

I remember one draft in particular which joined us at Choques in March 1915 and 75 per cent. of whom were returned to the Base within a week as medically unfit. I should say that the majority of our drafts after 1st December were only partially trained.

                        Yours sincerely,
                (Signed)   J.D. Boyd.

XORPS TROOPS

File with 3rd Brigade.
1st Division.

1st BATTALION

THE QUEEN'S ROYAL WEST SURREY REGIMENT

DECEMBER 1 9 1 4

1st Division
2nd Inf. Bde.

CORPS TROOPS from 8/11/14.

WAR DIARY

(QUEEN'S) 1st Bn. The R.WEST SURREY REG.

DECEMBER
1914

WAR DIARY
or
INTELLIGENCE SUMMARY.
(Erase heading not required.)

Army Form C. 2118.

Hour, Date, Place	Summary of Events and Information	Remarks and references to Appendices
HAZEBROUCK		
December 1st & 2nd	Ordinary Routine	Lt Boyd & Lt D. & Mr Walker returned from leave.
Dec 3rd	The Batt paraded at 6.30 a.m. for the King's visit, and formed a guard of Honor of 100 R & F under Lieut BOYD. H.M. The King inspected the guard. Amongst these were 83 original members of the Batt who had not left England with the Batt in August.	
Dec 4th & 5th	Ordinary Routine	
Dec 6th	Some bombs dropped by hostile aeroplanes where caused several casualties among the L.N. Lancashire Regt and civilians	
Dec 7th	Route March at 9.15 am	Lieut A. A. BRADSHAW joined the Batt
Dec 8th	Ordinary Routine	
" 9th		
" 10th		
" 11th		
" 12th		Capt P. C. ESDAILE joined the Batt at 9.30 p.m. Capt M. G. HEATH " " "

WAR DIARY or INTELLIGENCE SUMMARY.

Army Form C. 2118.

Hour, Date, Place	Summary of Events and Information	Remarks and references to Appendices
HAZEBROUCK		
13th December	Divine service at 11 am in the Barrie.	
14"	Orders issued confidentially at 9 am that the 2nd & 3rd Army Corps are commencing an attack on the line LE TOUQUET – WARNETON – HOLLEBEKE Kw 17 A C and Indian Corps Divn to be in reserve and ready to move off at 2 hours notice.	8th Divn OSTEND MAP
15"	Ordinary Routine. All officers fired practice from during the afternoon for instruction. Lieut WALSH R.A.M.C. joined 1st Bn for duty. Ordinary Routine. The Rev J. BLACKBOURNE (Senr Chaplain 1st A.C. joined)	1/2
16"	"	
17"	"	
18"	2nd 3rd & 4th Corps will relieve Corps now attacking at 10 a m 1st Corps in Reserve & ready to move off at 2 hours notice.	
19"	Ordinary Routine.	
20"	Divine service at 11 am in the Barrie.	
21"	The first Divn left this neighbourhood this morning. Bremen arms to be ready to move at 7 a m tomorrow.	J. H. S. Capt

WAR DIARY
INTELLIGENCE SUMMARY

Army Form C. 2118.

Hour, Date, Place	Summary of Events and Information	Remarks and references to Appendices
HAZEBROUCK.		
22nd Dec. HINGES.	Orders to move cancelled at 7.15 A.M. and altered for 7 A.M. tomorrow	
23rd Dec.	Marched off at 7 A.M. via MERVILLE & HINGES. Reached the latter at 12.30 p.m. & went into billets.	ST OMER MAP and ARRAS MAP.
24th Dec.	Cleaning up billets & moved into some huts vac. [Heavy rain - officials] 1/2 Lt.-Col. D.T. PELL sick under an operation in hospital of the German XV Corps on 20 + 21st. 2nd Lieut C.B. BROOKE joined with 156 3 CO's men (9th Reinforcement.)	Present strength (Batt": vis:- 17 Officers (includes 2 attached) 435 men (includes 12 attached)
25th Dec.	Open air service at 10.30 a.m. Cards recvd & distributed from Princess Mary. Their Majesties. also present. Princess Mary.	
26th Dec.	Ordinary Routine. Capt. R.L.G. Heath and 2nd Lieuts M.L.B. Howell, B.M. PICKERING (Buffs) and W.L.T. NICHOLAS (Buffs) joined the Bat".	General Kelly - Kenny (Hin Col f/Regt) and Army at Brigade.
27th Dec.	Divn dinner in open air at 10.30 A.M. Capt J.D. BOYD awarded the D.S.O. by the C. in C.	
28th Dec.	Captain R.L.G. HEATH paraded at 8.30 A.M. with a detachment of 46 2 CO's & men & proceeded to KILLERS	Capt (ARRAS MAP)

WAR DIARY
or
INTELLIGENCE SUMMARY.

(Erase heading not required.)

Army Form C. 2118.

Hour, Date, Place	Summary of Events and Information	Remarks and references to Appendices
HINGES.		
29th Dec.	To act as Army Troops.	
30th Dec.	Ordinary Routine. C.O. inspected BETHUNE detachment in the afternoon. Lieuts O.V. LE BAS, P.R.O. TRENCH and J.B. CLOSE joined the Bn.	
31st	Ordinary Routine. Lieut A. BURTON & 2nd Lieut J.D. COLEBROOK (5th Inniskillings) joined.	[signature] GMO's Copy 1/2

www.ingramcontent.com/pod-product-compliance
Lightning Source LLC
Chambersburg PA
CBHW081445160426
43193CB00013B/2389